CAMILLE SAINT-SAËNS

ORATORIO DE NOËL

Weihnachtsoratorium / Christmas Oratorio

für Soli, Chor, Harfe, Orgel und Streicher
for Soloists, Chorus, Harp, Organ and Strings

Opus 12

Neuausgabe nach den Quellen von
New edition based on original sources by

Edward Blakeman

Klavierauszug von / Vocal Score by

Roland Erben

EIGENTUM DES VERLEGERS · ALLE RECHTE VORBEHALTEN
ALL RIGHTS RESERVED

C. F. PETERS

FRANKFURT/M. · LEIPZIG · LONDON · NEW YORK

INHALT / CONTENTS

Vorwort / Preface . . . . III/IV

1. Prélude (Dans le style de Séb. Bach) 2

2. Récit et Chœur
   Recit (Soli: Soprano, Contralto, Ténor, Baryton) 4
   Chœur 8

3. Air 11
   (Mezzo-Soprano solo)

4. Air avec Chœur 14
   (Ténor solo, Chœur)

5. Duo 17
   (Soli: Soprano, Baryton)

6. Chœur 22

7. Trio 28
   (Soli: Soprano, Ténor, Baryton)

8. Quatuor 38
   (Soli: Soprano, Mezzo-Soprano, Contralto, Baryton)

9. Quintette et Chœur 43
   (Soli: Soprano, Mezzo-Soprano, Contralto, Ténor, Baryton)

10. Chœur 54

BESETZUNG / ORCHESTRATION
Arpa – Organo
Violino I – Violino II – Viola – Violoncello – Contrabbasso
Soli: Soprano – Mezzo-Soprano – Alto – Tenore – Baritono
Coro

Aufführungsdauer / Duration: ca. 40 Min.

Partitur / Full Score EP 11052
Aufführungsmaterial leihweise und käuflich erhältlich
Orchestral material is available for hire and purchase

Vorwort

Komposition und Aufführung

Saint-Saëns war 23 Jahre alt, als er sein *Oratorio de Noël* (Weihnachtsoratorium) schrieb. Das Werk enthält die ganze Frische eines jungen Künstlers, der danach strebte, sich als Komponist weiter zu profilieren. Seit gerade einem Jahr hatte Saint-Saëns die Organistenstelle an der berühmten Église de la Madeleine in Paris inne, und das Oratorium entstand als größeres Unterfangen anlässlich seines zweiten Weihnachtsfestes in diesem begehrten Amt. In lediglich zwölf Tagen zwischen dem 4. und 15. Dezember 1858 niedergeschrieben, war das Oratorium ursprünglich sechssätzig konzipiert, so wie dies im Folgenden aus den fett hervorgehobenen Nummern 1, 2, 3, 5, 8 und 10 des endgültigen Werks ersichtlich wird:

1. **Prélude**
2. **Récit et chœur**
3. **Air**
4. Air avec chœur
5. **Duo**
6. Chœur
7. Trio
8. **Quatuor**
9. Quintette et chœur
10. **Chœur**

Der ersten, noch sechssätzigen Fassung gab Saint-Saëns den lateinischen Titel *Oratorium pro nocte Nativitatis Christi* und sah darin Solopartien für jeweils eine Sopran-, Mezzosopran-, Alt-, Tenor- und Baritonstimme sowie einen vierstimmigen Chor, Orgel und Streichquartett vor. In dieser Besetzung wurde das Stück in der Madeleine während der Feierlichkeiten zum 1. Weihnachtstag 1858 uraufgeführt.

Für eine weitere Aufführung (deren Datum unbekannt ist) fügte Saint-Saëns zwei Harfen im unisono hinzu, die einigen Abschnitten der Orgelstimme im *Duo* eine zusätzliche Farbe verleihen. Er begann auch, das Werk zu erweitern, sehr wahrscheinlich kam zunächst die *Air* für Tenor hinzu – diejenige Solostimme, der er in der Originalversion nur 14 Takte eines Rezitativs gegeben hatte –, und außerdem beendete er diesen neuen Satz mit einem Chor (Nr. 4 der endgültigen Fassung). Es folgten die Sätze 6, 7 und 9; zudem fügte Saint-Saëns in den Nr. 7 und 9 eine Harfenstimme hinzu (die er später in den Korrekturfahnen zum Erstdruck noch einmal revidierte). Weiterhin setzte er eine Kontrabassstimme hinzu, welche an verschiedenen Stellen die Cellostimme verdoppelt und so dem gesamten Orchesterklang eine neue Dimension gibt.

Das *Oratorio de Noël*, so benannte Saint-Saëns die zehnsätzige Fassung neu, ist zwar ein Jugendwerk, aber eines, für das er zeitlebens eine tiefe Zuneigung behielt. Es war sein erster größerer Erfolg, mit dem er seine Fähigkeit, für Solisten, Chor und Orchester komponieren zu können, überzeugend unter Beweis stellte. Die Originalpartitur enthält nicht nur untrügliche Anzeichen für seine überaus akribische Arbeitsweise sowie seine Klarheit in der Erfindung, sondern lässt auch seinen besonderen Sinn für Humor und Fantasie erkennen: Zum Beispiel bediente sich Saint-Saëns in Takt 87 des *Récit et Chœur* zu Beginn der komplizierten Vokalfuge einer falschen Wendung. Nach acht Takten brach er ab, strich die ganze Passage fein säuberlich aus und zeichnete darüber einen Engel mit züngelnden Flammen über seinem Haupt!

Saint-Saëns selbst wählte die biblischen Texte sorgfältig aus. Verschiedene Stellen lassen erkennen, wie sehr ihm daran gelegen war, die musikalische Betonung exakt mit jener der Wörter in Übereinstimmung zu bringen; nicht selten nahm er während der Ausarbeitung noch Änderungen vor. Stilistisch orientierte sich Saint-Saëns in seinem Oratorium an den Kirchenkantaten Johann Sebastian Bachs (mit der Motette *Veni Creator* hatte er im Laufe des Jahres 1858 schon einmal eine ähnliche Hommage an Palestrina komponiert), doch ist seine musikalische Sprache durchaus eigenständig zu nennen. Nach dem einleitenden *Prélude* schließt sich die Weihnachtsgeschichte in Rezitativen an, gefolgt von einer Reihe von Arien und Ensemblestücken, welche das Wunder der Menschwerdung reflektieren. Das Werk wird abgerundet durch einen Chor, der in der Art eines aufrüttelnden lutheranischen Chorals erklingt.

In seiner endgültigen Fassung fand das Weihnachtsoratorium schließlich auch den Weg in den Konzertsaal, wo es dank mächtiger vokaler und instrumentaler Kraftentfaltung trotz seines begrenzten Instrumentariums einen imposanten Eindruck hinterlässt. Gleichwohl lohnt ein Seitenblick auch auf die bescheidenere sechssätzige Erstfassung, welche mit ihrer friedvollen Empfindsamkeit und ihrer Intimität der Gemeinde an jenem 1. Weihnachtstag im Jahre 1858 sehr gefallen haben dürfte. Diese erste Fassung ist es durchaus wert, erinnert und vielleicht innerhalb eines liturgischen oder auch anderen Rahmens aufgeführt zu werden – es handelt sich mithin um ein Werk im Werk.

Publikationsgeschichte

Das *Oratorio de Noël* wurde zum ersten Mal in Paris um das Jahr 1863 vom Verleger G. Flaxland im Klavierauszug veröffentlicht. Der Klaviersatz stammte von einem Schüler Saint-Saëns', dem Organisten Eugène Gigout. Möglicherweise existierte auch eine gedruckte Partitur, doch konnte ein entsprechendes Exemplar nicht ermittelt werden.

Einige Jahre später gab Flaxlands Nachfolger A. Durand eine Partitur heraus, die allerdings undatiert blieb, und legte auch den Klavierauszug neu auf. Saint-Saëns nutzte diese Gelegenheit, in seinen Originalmanuskripten verschiedene Änderungen und Zusätze anzubringen, außerdem überarbeitete er die Rezitative im zweiten Satz, um die Textbehandlung weiter zu verfeinern. Nun wurde für das Werk auch eine Widmung vergeben, nämlich an Vicomtesse Clémence de Grandval, eine Schülerin des Komponisten.

Trotz aller Bemühungen von Saint-Saëns, die Publikation des Oratoriums zu überwachen, finden sich im Erstdruck viele Fehler und Auslassungen. Die vorliegende Neuausgabe versucht diese Defizite zu beheben und durch Vergleiche mit verschiedenen Manuskriptquellen das Werk zum ersten Mal in einer den Intentionen Saint-Saëns' so nahe wie möglich kommenden Weise darzustellen. Dort, wo weiterhin Unklarheiten bestehen, weisen eckige Klammern auf alternative oder ungesicherte Lesarten hin. Dies gilt besonders für jene kleineren Details, die in der gedruckten Ausgabe auftauchten, jedoch in der von Saint-Saëns selbst korrigierten handschriftlichen Stichvorlage nicht vorhanden waren.

Zur vorliegenden Ausgabe

Der von Roland Erben neu erarbeitete Klavierauszug zielt auf klangvolle Wiedergabe des Orchesters unter Berücksichtigung der pianistischen Ausführbarkeit. Bei technisch schwierigen Passagen wie im *Trio* Nr. 7 wurden Fingersätze hinzugefügt. Die Grundlage für den Notentext bildet die zugehörige Partiturausgabe (Edition Peters Nr. 11052), in der auch der Revisionsbericht mit detaillierten Angaben zu den benutzten Quellen enthalten ist. Neben der historischen, bereits für den Durand-Erstdruck verwendeten Stichvorlage mit handschriftlichen Korrekturen von Saint-Saëns wurde erstmals auch das erhaltene Partiturautograph herangezogen. Die genannten Quellen befinden sich in der Musikabteilung der Bibliothèque Nationale in Paris.

Mein Dank gilt den Mitarbeitern der Musikabteilung der Bibliothèque Nationale sowie Yves Gérard, dem profunden Saint-Saëns-Kenner, mit dem ich viele anregende Gespräche über diesen faszinierenden Komponisten führen konnte.

London, März 2008 *Edward Blakeman*
(Übersetzung: Anja Bühnemann)

Preface

Composition and Performance

Saint-Saëns was twenty-three when he wrote his *Oratorio de Noël* (Christmas Oratorio) and it has all the freshness of a young composer eager to prove himself. He had been organist of the fashionable Church of the Madeleine in Paris for just a year – a prestigious position – and the *Oratorio* was a major undertaking for his second Christmas there. Written in just twelve days between 4 and 15 December 1858, it was originally conceived in six movements, corresponding to no's 1, 2, 3, 5, 8, and 10 of the completed work highlighted below:

1. Prélude
2. Récit et chœur
3. Air
4. Air avec chœur
5. Duo
6. Chœur
7. Trio
8. Quatuor
9. Quintette et chœur
10. Chœur

Saint-Saëns gave this first version of the work the Latin title *Oratorium pro nocte Nativitatis Christi* and scored it for soprano, mezzo-soprano, contralto, tenor and baritone soloists, with four-part chorus, organ and string quartet. In this form it was first performed at the Madeleine during the celebrations on Christmas Day 1858.

For a subsequent performance (date unknown) Saint-Saëns had the idea of adding two harps in unison, doubling some sections of the organ part for extra colour in the *Duo*. He then began to expand the work, most likely initially with an *Air* for tenor – the solo voice which had been given only fourteen bars of recitative in the original version – and he completed this new movement with a chorus (No. 4 of the complete work). Movements 6, 7, and 9 then followed, and in 7 and 9 Saint-Saëns also included a single harp part (which he further revised at the proofs stage of the printed edition). He also added a double bass line to the strings, doubling the cello at various points and thus expanding the orchestral sound world of the whole work.

The *Oratorio de Noël* (as Saint-Saëns renamed the ten-movement version) was indeed a youthful work, but one for which he retained a great affection – his first major success at writing convincingly for soloists, chorus and orchestra. The original score bears not only the hallmarks of his meticulous approach and clarity of invention, but also of his sense of humour and fantasy: for example, at bar 87 of the *Récit et Chœur* he took a wrong turning as he started to construct an elaborate vocal fugue. After eight bars he gave it up, lightly crossed-out the whole section and superimposed a sketch of a winged angel with a tongue of fire above his head!

Saint-Saëns carefully selected the Biblical texts himself, and struggled in various places to get the musical stress of the words exactly right, several times changing his mind. For the general style of the *Oratorio*, he turned to the example of J S Bach's church cantatas (he had paid a similar homage to Palestrina earlier in 1858 with a motet *Veni Creator*), although the actual musical language is very much his own. After an opening prelude, the Christmas story is told in recitative, and followed by a series of arias and ensembles which meditate on the mystery of the Incarnation. The work is rounded off with chorus which rings out like a stirring Lutheran chorale.

In its final form, the *Oratorio de Noël* has translated naturally to the concert hall, where it makes an imposing effect with large choral and orchestral forces. But it is worth remembering its more humble beginnings. The original six-movement version, with a small choir and chamber ensemble, has a pastoral delicacy and intimacy which must have delighted the congregation on Christmas Day 1858. Maybe this version is still worth considering as an option for liturgical (and other) performances – a work within a work.

Publication History

The *Oratorio de Noël* was published for the first time in Paris c. 1863 by G. Flaxland in a vocal score version (there may have been a full score but this has not been found), with a piano reduction by one of Saint-Saëns's students, the organist Eugène Gigout.

Some years later (the edition is undated), Flaxland's successor, A. Durand, published a full score and reissued the vocal score. At this point Saint-Saëns took the opportunity to make various revisions and additions to his original manuscripts, including some further rewriting of the recitatives in the second movement to improve the word setting. He dedicated the work to another of his students, the Vicomtesse Clémence de Grandval.

Despite Saint-Saëns's efforts, however, in overseeing the publication of the *Oratorio*, it had various mistakes and omissions. This new edition attempts to correct these, and by close comparison with the various manuscript sources to present the work for the first time in a form as close as possible to Saint-Saëns's intentions. Where there are still ambiguities, square brackets have been used to indicate alternative or uncertain readings – in particular for the inclusion of extra details that somehow appeared in the printed edition after the preparation and correction of Saint-Saëns final manuscript.

To the present Edition

Roland Erben's new piano reduction for this vocal score aims to reflect the orchestral sonorities while remaining comfortable and idiomatic to play. In technically difficult passages, e.g. in the *Trio* No 7, some fingerings have been added. The musical text is based on the associated edition in full score (Edition Peters No. 11052), which also contains a critical commentary with detailed notes on the sources. In addition to the manuscript, preserved with corrections and annotations by Saint-Saëns and used by Durand for the printed edition, we have also consulted for the first time the composer's autograph of the full score. These sources are housed in the Music Department of the Bibliothèque Nationale in Paris.

My grateful thanks go to the staff of the Music Department of the Bibliothèque Nationale and to the eminent Saint-Saëns authority, Yves Gérard, with whom I have shared many lively discussions about this most fascinating composer.

London, March 2008 *Edward Blakeman*

Oratorio de Noël

N° 1 Prélude

(Dans le style de Séb. Bach)

Camille Saint-Saëns (1835–1921)
opus 12
Herausgegeben von Edward Blakeman
Klavierauszug von Roland Erben

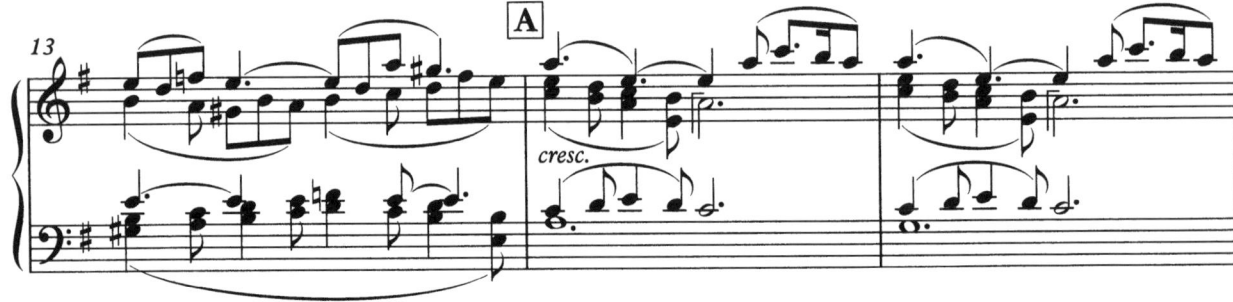

N° 2 Récit et Chœur

Soli: Soprano, Contralto, Ténor, Baryton

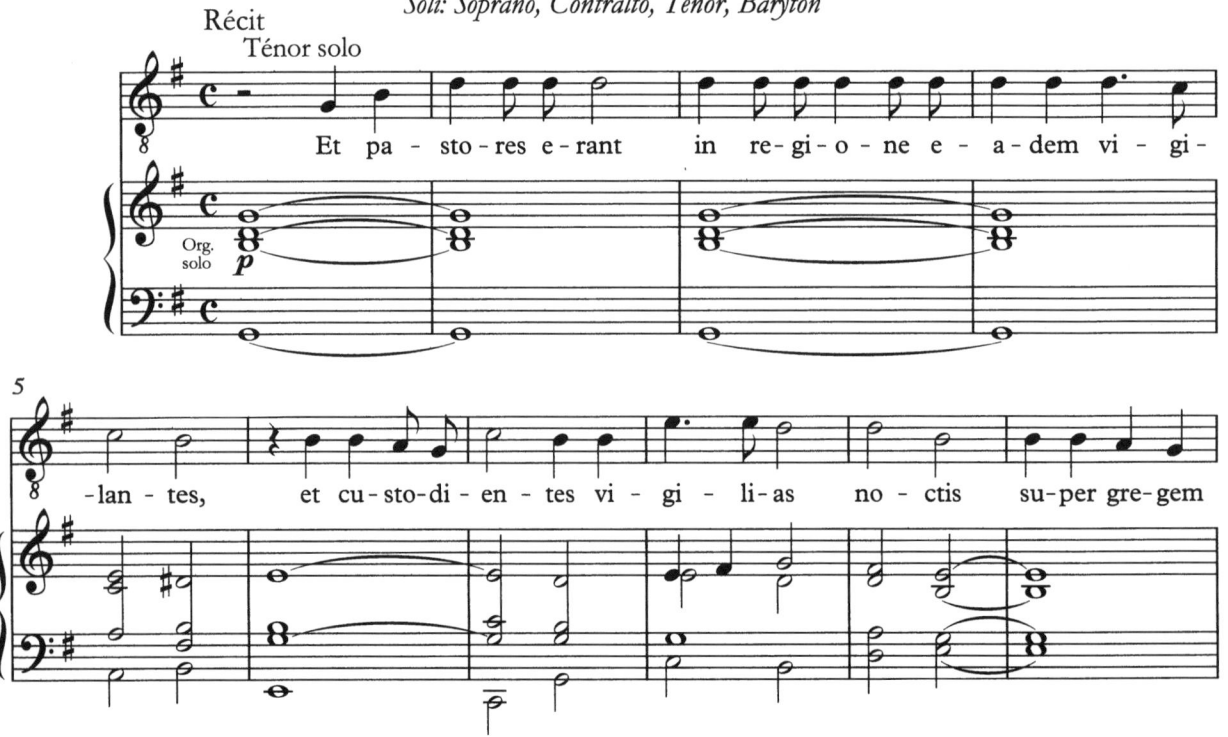

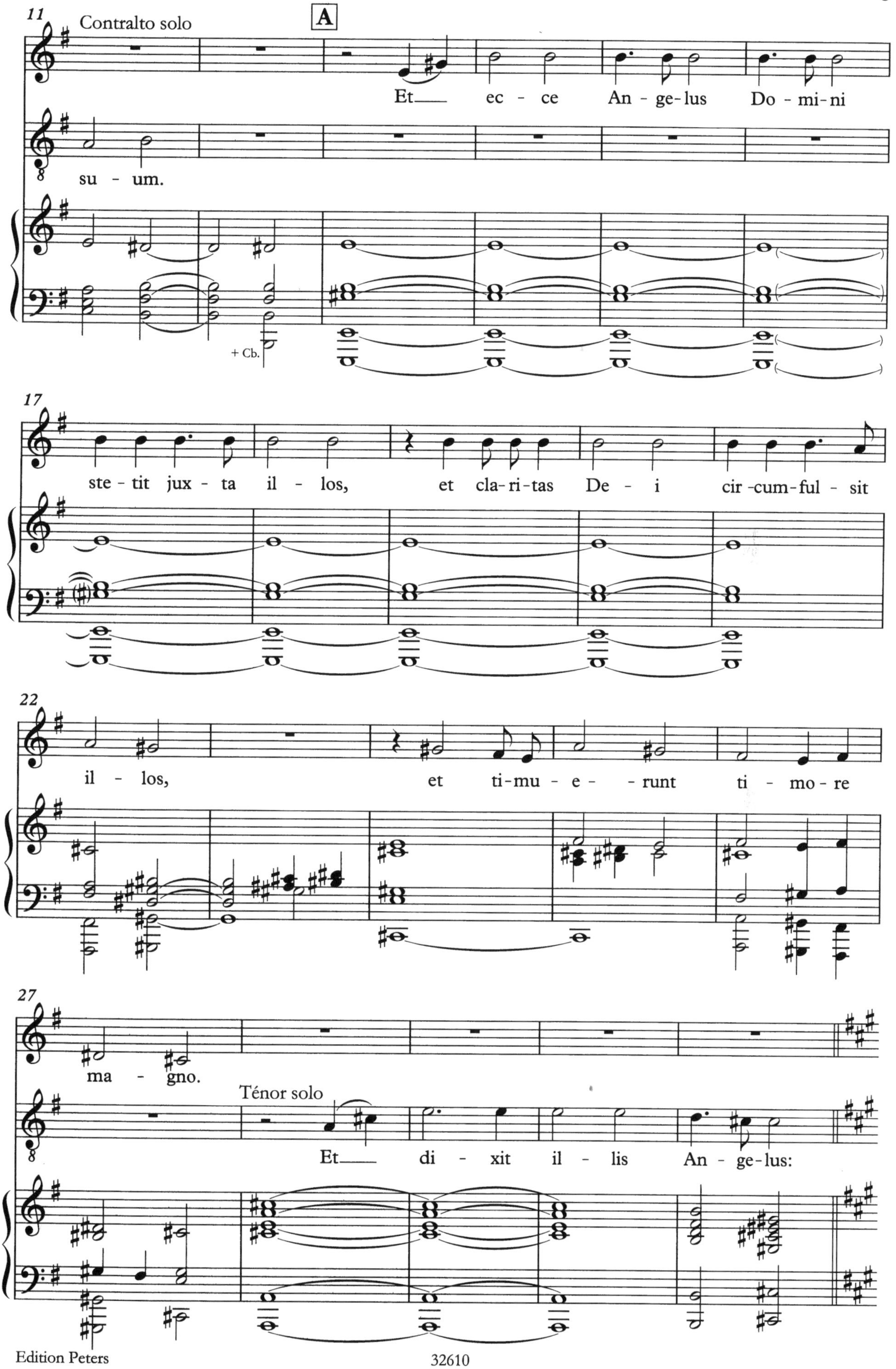
11
Contralto solo
A
Et ecce Angelus Domini
suum.
+ Cb.
17
stetit juxta illos, et claritas Dei circumfulsit
22
illos, et timuerunt timore
27
magno.
Ténor solo
Et dixit illis Angelus:

N° 3 Air

Mezzo-Soprano solo

N° 4 Air avec Chœur

Ténor solo

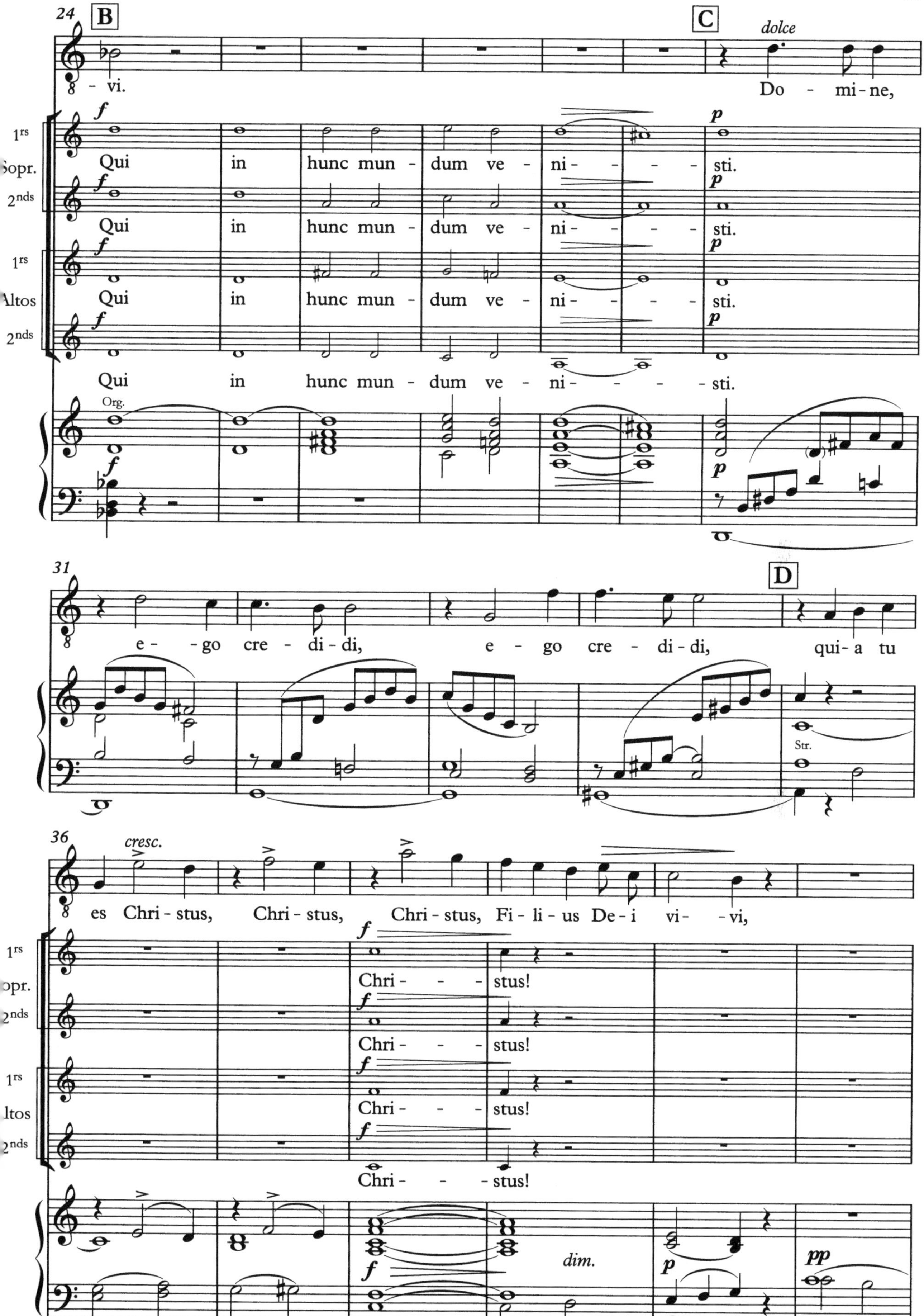
24
B
C
dolce
vi. Do - mi - ne,
1rs
Sopr.
2nds
Qui in hunc mun - dum ve - ni - - - - sti.
1rs
Altos
2nds
Org.
31
D
e - go cre - di - di, e - go cre - di - di, qui - a tu
Str.
36
cresc.
es Chri - stus, Chri - stus, Chri - stus, Fi - li - us De - i vi - - vi,
Chri - - - stus!
dim.

N° 5 Duo

Soli: Soprano, Baryton

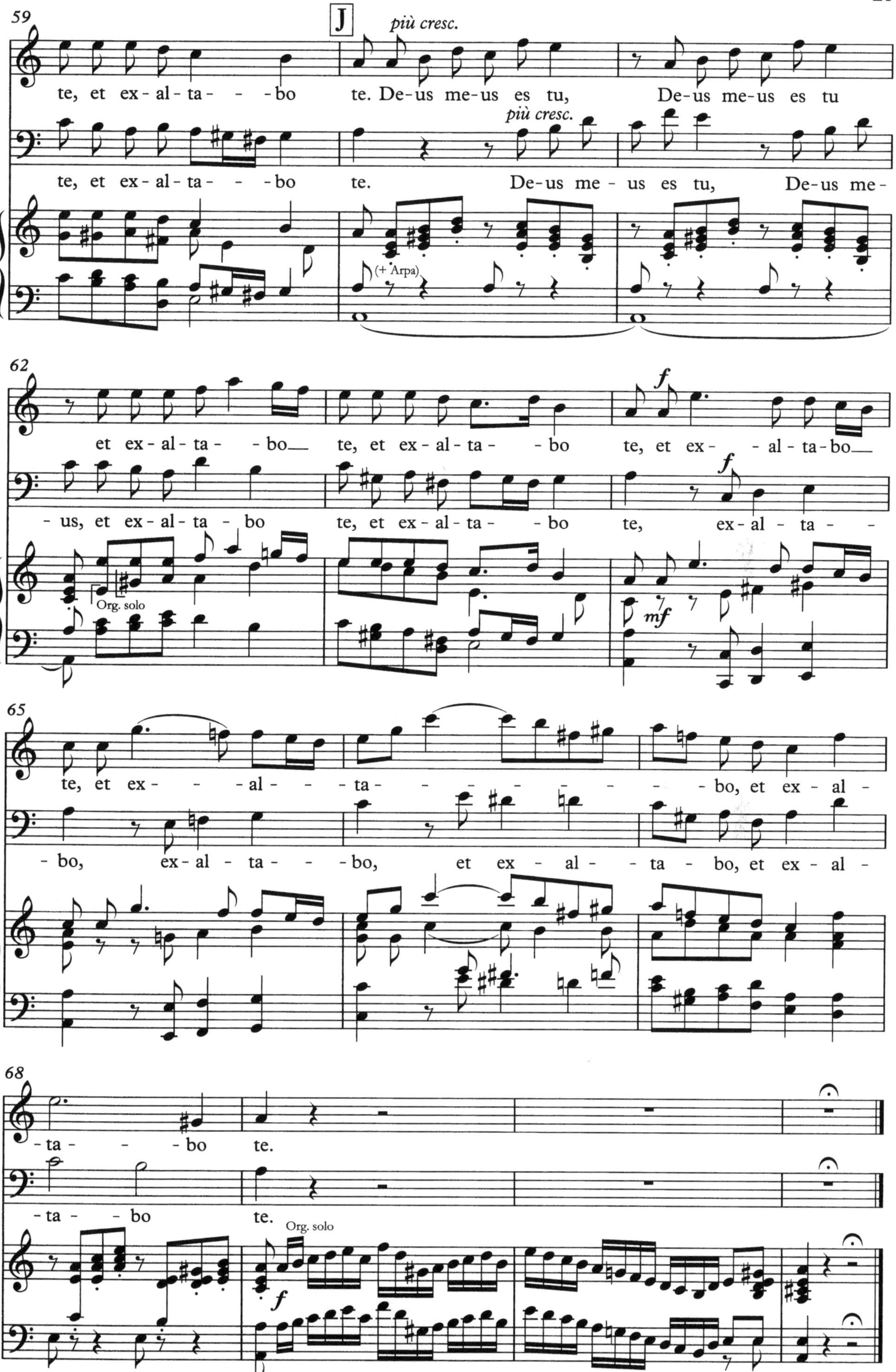
59
J
più cresc.
te, et ex-al-ta- - bo te. De-us me-us es tu, De-us me-us es tu
più cresc.
te, et ex-al-ta- - bo te. De-us me - us es tu, De-us me-
(+ Arpa)
62
f
et ex-al-ta- - bo te, et ex-al-ta- - bo te, et ex- - al-ta-bo
f
- us, et ex-al-ta - bo te, et ex-al-ta- - bo te, ex-al-ta-
Org. solo
mf
65
te, et ex- - al- - ta- - - - - - - - bo, et ex-al-
- bo, ex-al-ta- - - bo, et ex - al- - ta - bo, et ex-al-
68
- ta- - - bo te.
- ta- - bo te.
Org. solo
f

N° 7 Trio

Soli: Soprano, Ténor, Baryton

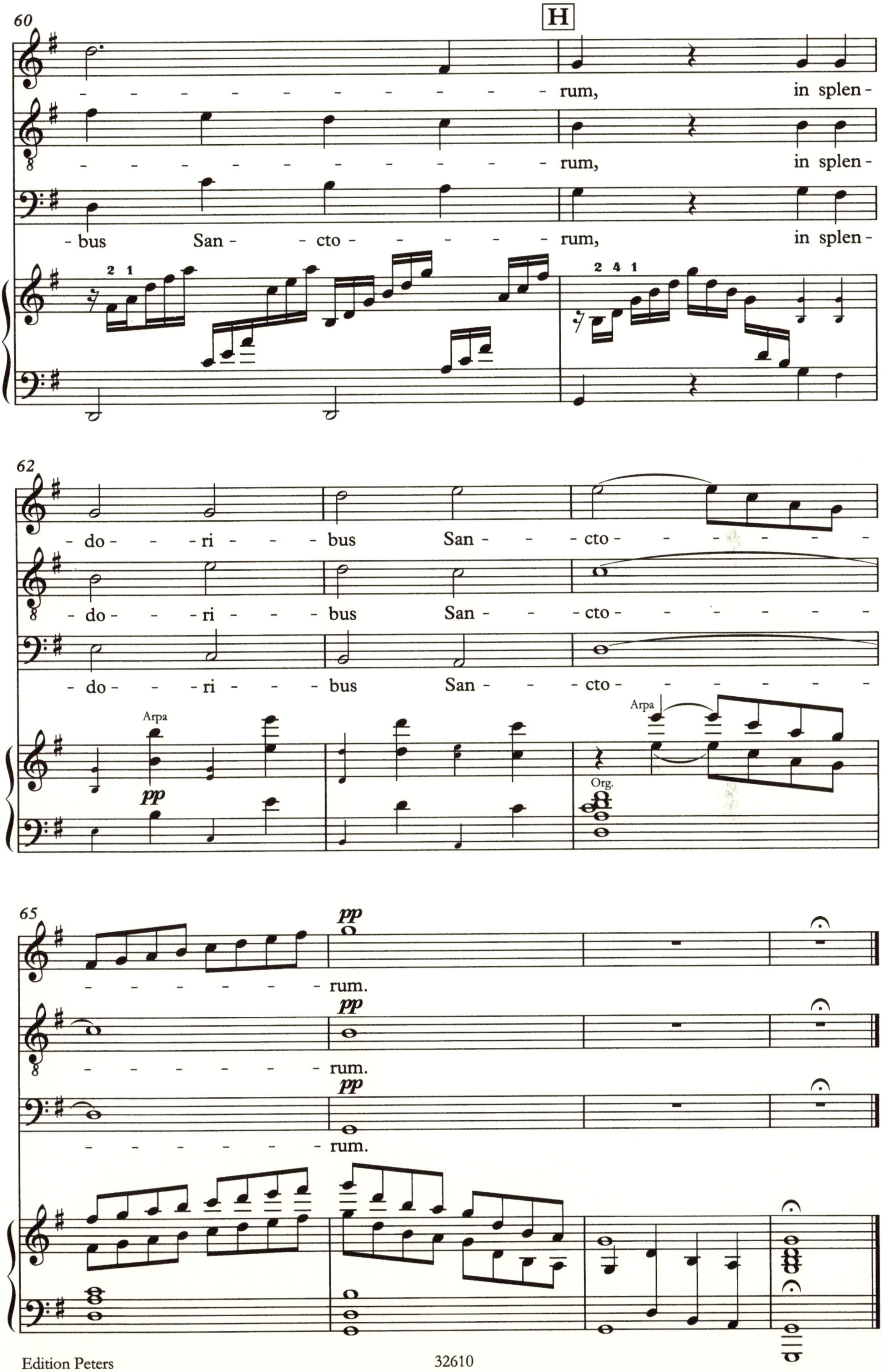
60
H
rum, in splen-
rum, in splen-
bus San - cto - rum, in splen-
2 1
2 4 1
62
do - ri - bus San - cto -
do - ri - bus San - cto -
do - ri - bus San - cto -
Arpa
pp
Org.
65
pp
rum.
pp
rum.
pp
rum.

N° 8 Quatuor

Soli: Soprano, Mezzo-Soprano, Contralto, Baryton

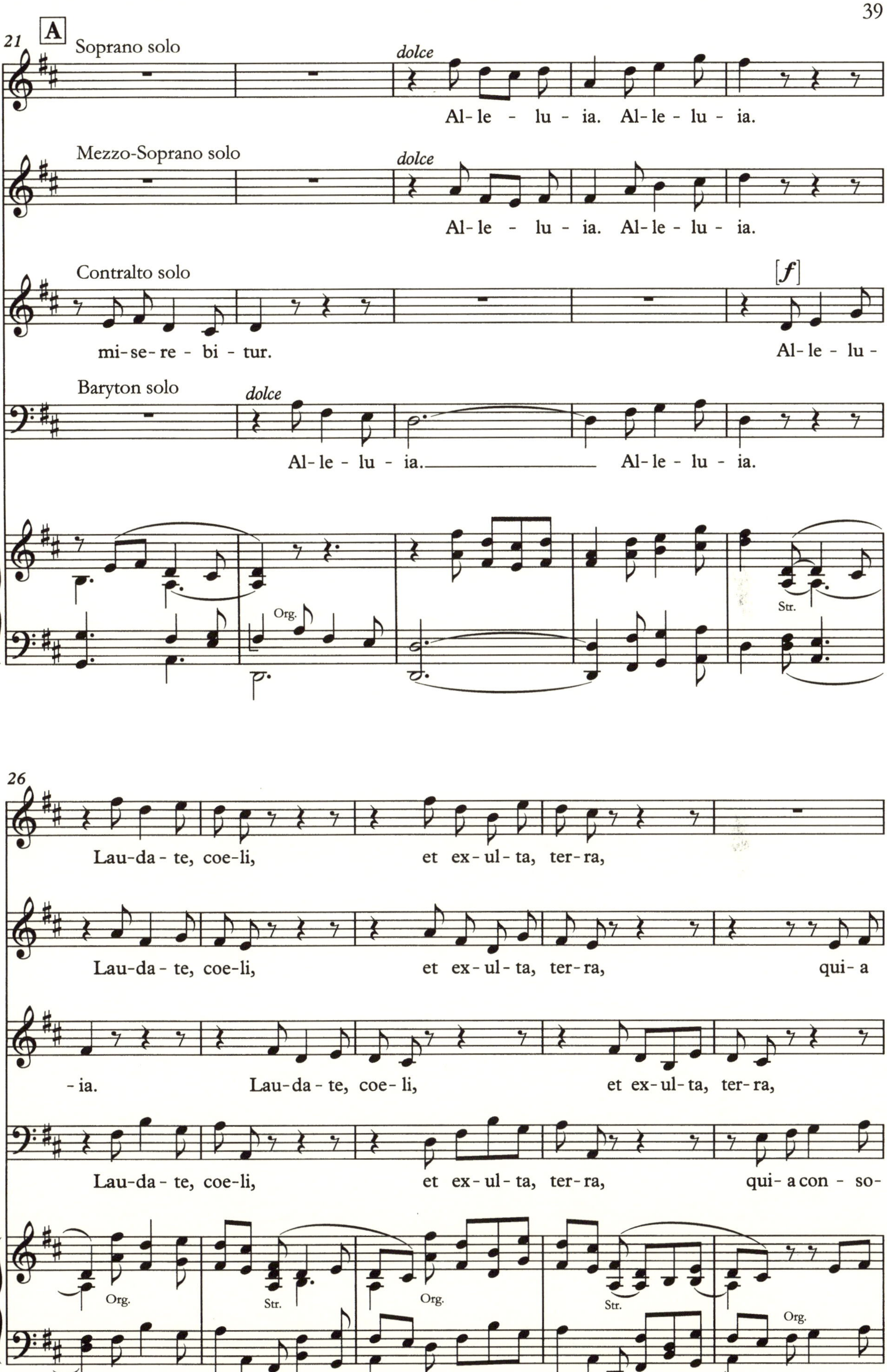
21
A
Soprano solo
dolce
Al- le - lu - ia. Al- le - lu - ia.
Mezzo-Soprano solo
dolce
Al- le - lu - ia. Al- le - lu - ia.
Contralto solo
[f]
mi- se- re - bi - tur.
Al- le - lu -
Baryton solo
dolce
Al- le - lu - ia. Al- le - lu - ia.
Org.
Str.
26
Lau-da - te, coe-li, et ex- ul - ta, ter - ra,
Lau-da - te, coe-li, et ex- ul - ta, ter - ra, qui- a
- ia. Lau- da - te, coe- li, et ex- ul - ta, ter - ra,
Lau-da - te, coe-li, et ex- ul - ta, ter - ra, qui- a con - so-
Org.
Str.
Org.
Str.
Org.

N° 9 Quintette et Chœur

Soli: Soprano, Mezzo-Soprano, Contralto, Ténor, Baryton

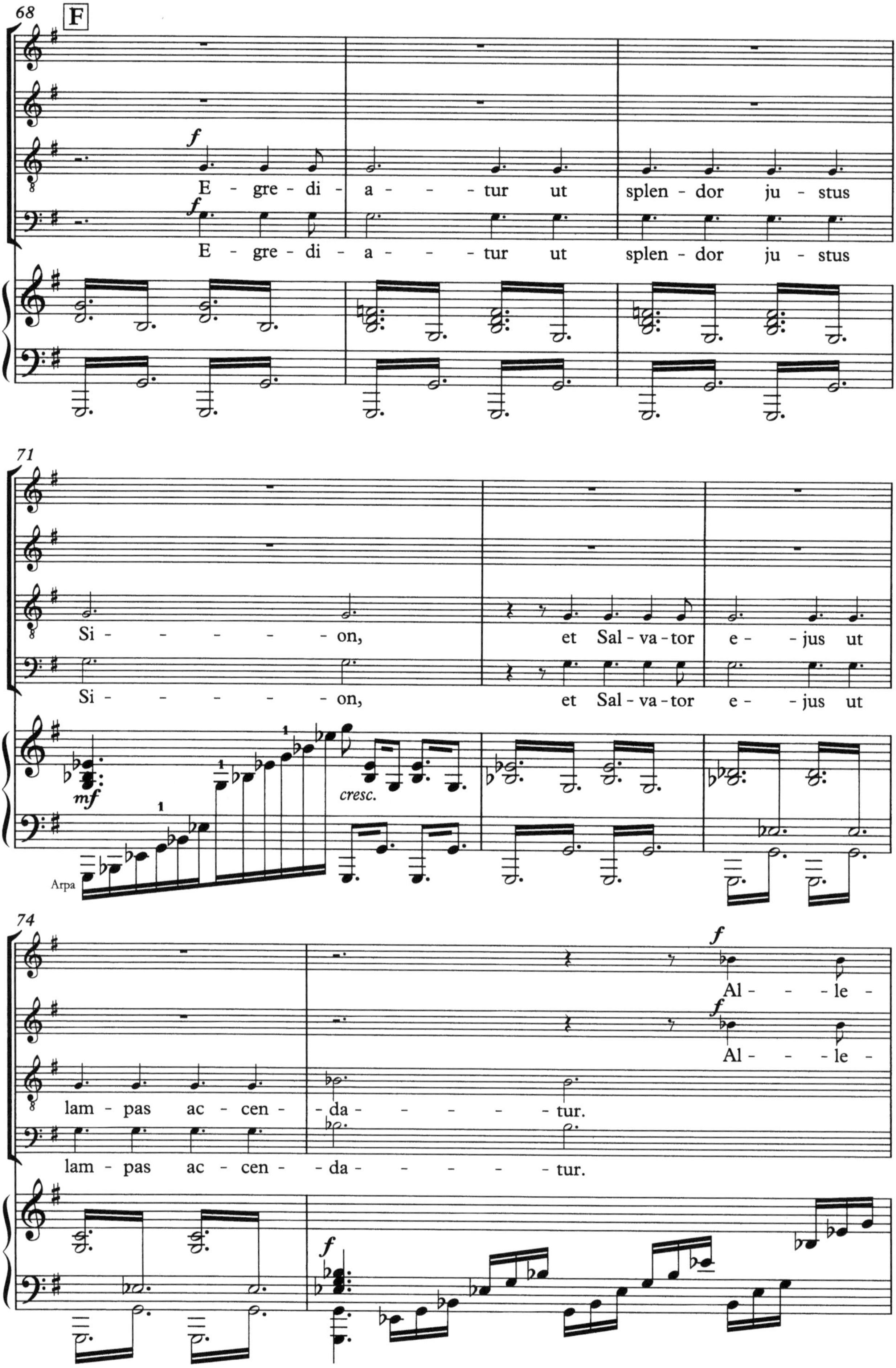
68
F
E - gre - di - a - tur ut splen - dor ju - stus
E - gre - di - a - tur ut splen - dor ju - stus
71
Si - on, et Sal - va - tor e - jus ut
Si - on, et Sal - va - tor e - jus ut
mf
cresc.
Arpa
74
Al - le -
Al - le -
lam - pas ac - cen - da - tur.
lam - pas ac - cen - da - tur.

Nº 10 Chœur

EDITION PETERS

CHORSINGEN – LEICHT GEMACHT

JOHANN SEBASTIAN BACH
- Johannes-Passion BWV 245
  Klavierauszug EP 8635
  CD: MPC 8635-1/2/3/4 (je 2 CDs)
- Matthäus-Passion BWV 244
  Klavierauszug EP 4503
  CD: MPC 4503-1/2/3/4 (je 2 CDs)
- Messe h-Moll BWV 232
  Klavierauszug EP 8736
  CD für S1 / S2 / A / T / B:
  MPC 8736-11/12/2/3/4 (je 2 CDs)
- Weihnachtsoratorium BWV 248
  Klavierauszug EP 8719
  CD: MPC 8719-1/2/3/4 (je 2 CDs)

LUDWIG VAN BEETHOVEN
- 9. Symphonie / Chorfantasie c-Moll
  Klavierauszug 9. Symphonie EP 2227
  Klavierauszug Chorfantasie EP 8723
  CD: MPC 8723-1/2/3/4

JOHANNES BRAHMS
- Ein deutsches Requiem op. 45
  Klavierauszug EP 3672
  CD: MPC 3672-1/2/3/4 (je 2 CDs)

ANTONÍN DVOŘÁK
- Stabat Mater op. 58
  Klavierauszug EP 8639
  CD: MPC 8639-1/2/3/4 (je 2 CDs)

GABRIEL FAURÉ
- Requiem op. 48
  Klavierauszug EP 9562
  CD: MPC 9562-1/2/3/4

CHARLES GOUNOD
- Messe solennelle G-Dur (Cäcilienmesse)
  Klavierauszug EP 8729
  CD: MPC 8729-1/2/3/4

GEORG FRIEDRICH HÄNDEL
- Der Messias HWV 56
  (auf CD gesungen in deutsch)
  Klavierauszug EP 4501
  CD: MPC 4501-1/2/3/4 (je 2 CDs)

MPC Nr.: 1/2/3/4: 1=Sopran; 2=Alt; 3=Tenor; 4=Bass

JOSEPH HAYDN
- Die Schöpfung Hob. XXI: 2
  Klavierauszug EP 8998
  CD: MPC 66-1/2/3/4
- Die Jahreszeiten Hob. XXI: 3
  Klavierauszug EP 11031
  CD: MPC 11031-1/2/3/4

FELIX MENDELSSOHN BARTHOLDY
- Elias op. 70
  Klavierauszug EP 1749
  CD: MPC 1749-1/2/3/4 (je 2 CDs)
- 2. Symphonie (Lobgesang) B-Dur op. 52
  Klavierauszug EP 1750
  CD: MPC 1750-1/2/3/4
- Die erste Walpurgisnacht op. 60
  Klavierauszug EP 1752
  CD: MPC 1752-1/2/3/4
- Paulus op. 36
  Klavierauszug EP 1748
  CD: MPC 1748-1/2/3/4

WOLFGANG AMADEUS MOZART
- Missa C-Dur KV 317 (Krönungsmesse)
  Klavierauszug EP 8115
  CD: MPC 8115-1/2/3/4
- Requiem d-Moll KV 626 (Beyer)
  Klavierauszug EP 8700a
  CD: MPC 8700-1/2/3/4
- Missa c-Moll KV 427
  Klavierauszug EP 8706
  CD: MPC 8706-1/2/3/4

GIOACCHINO ROSSINI
- Petite Messe solennelle
  Partitur (=Klavierauszug) EP 8684
  CD: MPC 8684-1/2/3/4

FRANZ SCHUBERT
- Messe G-Dur D 167
  Klavierauszug EP 10858
  CD: MPC 1049-1/2/3/4

GIUSEPPE VERDI
- Requiem
  Klavierauszug EP 4251
  CD: MPC 4251-1/2/3/4 (je 2 CDs)

musicPartner

C. F. Peters · Frankfurt/M. · Leipzig · London · New York
www.edition-peters.de